Poems for the Advisory Committee
on Antarctic Names

Dearest Evalyn,
true, wise, steadfast
friend. I'm so glad you slipped
me that note at The Nightwood Theatre
Studio so many years ago. Thank you
for sharing this journey with me.

love always,

SORAYA PEERBAYE

Poems for the Advisory Committee on Antarctic Names

Edited by Roo Borson.
Cover image: *Ice shelf edge with snow drift,* © Staphy | Dreamstime.com.
Back cover image and all interior images © Yousouf Peerbaye.
Cover design and interior page design by Julie Scriver.
Printed in Canada on paper containing 100% post-consumer fibre.
10 9 8 7 6 5 4 3 2 1

Library and Archives Canada Cataloguing in Publication

Peerbaye, Soraya, 1971-
    Poems for the Advisory Committee on Antarctic Names / Soraya Peerbaye.

ISBN 978-0-86492-536-7

    I. Title.

PS8631.E395P64 2009   C811'.6   C2009-901743-1

Goose Lane Editions acknowledges the financial support of the Canada Council for the Arts, the Government of Canada through the Book Publishing Industry Development Program (BPIDP), and the New Brunswick Department of Wellness, Culture, and Sport for its publishing activities.

Goose Lane Editions
Suite 330, 500 Beaverbrook Court
Fredericton, New Brunswick
CANADA E3B 5X4
www.gooselane.com

Pour mes parents
et mes frères

and for Mark
and Sheyla

By starting the story, the story tells you; tells you
how to go on and how to look back
— Marilyn Dumont

Contents

South coast, Mauritius

South coast, Mauritius

arc of water rising from the car wheels, translucent ribs
lifting as we plough through rivulets left by storm;
in the streets, young men, brown ankles bangled by sunlight
and rainwater. At Gris-Gris, where we walk the basalt shore,
a girl in a green salwar kameez, turned verdant kite
as she runs in salt-arrowed wind; above, seabirds, swept
as Arabic calligraphy. Graffiti by the crumbling stone kiosk
exposing its skeleton of rust at Pointe-aux-Roches
      Ramesh love Primila
                 while my small brother, clambering
over tide pools, holds up a starfish, his whole body
starfish as he loses, catches his balance, dances unsteady
      on one foot. But mostly, these
velocity-painted images, as we drive along the coast, me
cyclopean with my eye to the viewfinder: filao trees, fragile
sentinels, overexposed by coral light pouring through late
afternoon, their rows and rows interrupting the slow sun like
frames of film caught in eager machinery, my finger never fast
enough to release the shutter, as I try to photograph
the light, the light photographs me

Curios: Poems for K.

Zistoire

I've learned that the story comes from the invitation to come in.
The embrace, his cheek against mine, the stubbled feel of a sun-
hollowed sea urchin. He leaves his shoes at the door, hangs
his coat on the banister; I put on the kettle. The story comes
from the invitation to stay.

His hands, bronze, dark green filigree of veins. His voice,
warm, the timbre of wood.

We talk of family, his patients, horse-racing, poetry, cooking,
dreaming or not dreaming. Small words nod their heads, my *huh*,
hmm, Créole utterances that have found their way into our mouths
from French and Arabic, Urdu and Hindi, Malagasy.
Ayo, taé, y'Allah . . .

Sometimes, most often when we talk of music, or matters
musical — a concert he attended, how he learned to play
the harmonica, Dr. Oliver Sacks' lecture on music and the brain —
his voice seizes. I've learned to make my attention
gentle, then, to listen without hurry, to pretend not to notice
his glistening eye.

Pistasse

between us, on the kitchen table:
two cups of tea, pistachios.

in the bowl, their abundance,
their crackling anecdotes: our

hands, absent-minded, kindling
this light green warmth.

how we recognize each other
in gesture: his shrug, bargaining

at the bazaar with mamzelle
pomme d'amour, missié pistasse;

or hunchbacked theft from the bulk
bins, marked NO SAMPLING

(not theft, he protests, but critique
of an economic system — in a nutshell).

treble *crack!* of tooth, husk, kernel,
shucks red-stuccoed tidbit,

coaxes it out; brown-feathered
rooster, jiggles it

into gullet; guzzles his tea (sibilant
stream, glottal gulps).

mm, he says, charmed
as sweetness washes lemony salt;

dusts his palms with a small flourish,
smiles: extravagant teeth.

Disque

A boy with whole-bodied intent,
      he'd snatched the 78 rpm
   from the Morning Glory gramophone,

      shattered it: shining blue-black shards
at his feet. This object, known first
   by its breaking.

A grown man, his fingers amble
      the dust jackets, the fine print
of their spines. A physical musing.

      Not the fumble for cassettes,
the noisy sputter and catch
   of sprockets in the deck's

mechanism. But this — the record held,
      by its edge, at an angle, shirt sleeve
salving the bruise of fingerprints. *Écoute,*

      he says. We sit in the living room, as the needle
passes through its brief darkness, a cyclical,
   crackly creek. We tilt our heads back.

His favourites restored, iridescent on compact discs,
      but he rarely plays them, can't bear
   their breathless perfection,

     misses the scratch, skip and stutter,
that sent us into laughing fits.
     Or perhaps

it's the gesture itself,
     the needle carried to the record's surface,
a pond where the water ripples inwards.

Caméra

Thick, square fingers bunched at the small
mechanisms: deft, full of mind,
            fidgeting,

electronic trill and chitter responding
to gestures learned with Brownie,
bellows camera, Canonet, classic
            single-lens reflex —

            his boy's life in black and white,

                  my mother in Kodachrome — peacock-
                  blue saris, mustard-yellow
                        lenghas, psychedelic A-line skirts,

                  symmetry of landscapes —
                              clusters of guavas or Bing cherries,
                        fields of cane flower, fields of snow,

                  red canopy of flamboyants on the island,
                              October leaves in northern Ontario.

He stands huddled against the viewfinder,
holds his breath
            so the photograph will not blur,

snaps

then hurries, stiff stride,
                    lurching
          as he leans, kneels,
          gets down on belly and elbows.

Befuddled, slightly, by the new technology,
          the machine that thinks for his hands, but still,

such technical delight — swivel and twist,
          notch,   squint —

               in the photograph of a bird,
                    the amateur reflected —

grey-brown silhouette, his concentrated gesture, glossed
in the bird's eye.

Armonica

the span of a tamarind pod   full
of pulpy, puckering sound

untaught   he holds it backwards
so that this too   he reads from right   to left
learns *God Save the Queen*   then *Au clair de la lune*
theory slipping through the holes   save for the do, re, mi
of the Rodgers & Hammerstein mnemonic   (which he sings
in translation   *mi — la mie   d'un bon pain chaud!*)

in a Dublin concert hall   hears Larry Adler
melody an addled firefly   in cupped hands
the virtuoso tosses   Little Ladies   four-hole harmonicas
no bigger than two squares of chocolate   into the crowd

he catches one
grins a silver smile

chuffed (you could say)   and still, bashful   his amateur's repertoire
jazz   American musicals   *Alouette*
stinger of classical   *à la* Warner Brothers
and séga   first music he plays   for an audience
thirteen years old   the year of his grandmother's death
his mother and aunts gathered round

I can *see* this   as though I'd been there   he tucks the instrument
        in his palm   it disappears like a blade of grass
     hands, carinal   fingers, fluttering wings
foot tapping the kitchen floor   as the women murmur and clap
     Allé! Éta! Guette-li!   breaking the mourning period

        his grandfather drawn from the darkened bedroom
    to watch his cheeks fill and hollow
                    hollow
            to the shape of bone

                    inbreath and outbreath equal
                        bodied and living

Stéthescope

He quickens, takes my notebook, sketches a history
of the stethoscope:
   Laennec's monoaural, the early binaurals, and then
      a 1930's model — his father's —

ancestry gleaming in its metal cheekbones.

Heart sounds carried through India rubber and gutta-percha,
silk, precious woods and ivory;

            heart sounds through
               horn, bell, drum.

He remembers the physician's gesture, articulated
like the object's: angled,
            hinged and sprung in gawky formality;

how the eartips pinched his ears (he rubs his earlobes).

Until his first Littman. — *Génial,* he says. *Très joli.*
— *Joli?* I ask. What makes a stethoscope
      lovely?
      — *Ah* —

stainless steel, tygon tubing, single lumen
guiding sound from the glossy tympanum;
    the slight weight, the whole instrument
        only three ounces.
                — *Un son clair!* he exclaims,

    and in my mind the gesture
        lightens, loosens — his lean

over the patient, eyes closed or turned elsewhere,
as though he would be
    intimate but unintrusive. He disappears

into that listening,
    returns from it like someone surfacing;

teaches me heart sounds, lung sounds:
murmur, hum, crackle,
    the terrifying heave,
        arrhythmia of flutter and gallop,

thrill, the one he can feel
    through his fingertips.

Agram-bagram

I am looking for him, pen in hand, and a questionnaire I've devised
on the things of his boyhood: *Un objet de jeu?* I ask.
Un objet que tu collectionnais? Un souvenir? et cetera . . .

Marbles, of course.

Pop bottle caps, sun-glinted, rainbow
of rubber bands in a jar.

Yo-yos, made from spools of thread,
halved, swapped and sandwiched again.

A souvenir pen his father brought back from France:
his first view of Paris
thought-bubbled from the ink cartridge.

— *Pourquoi tu me demandes tout ça?*

I don't know. Because I believe in this, the object, quotidian,
beloved.
What our hands have held.

— *Allé*, I say, *continue* . . .

The rim of a coal tar drum to wheel through the city.
Il nous fallait être inventif, he says. Homemade spinning tops.

Like the ones you made for us, I ask, from lychee seeds
and a toothpick?
(Dark brown lustre of lychee seeds.)

No, no: whittled from a cylinder of wood,
a nail for a spine, a whip to crack them into higher speed.

He reads my poems, corrects them, describes the object again.
Il y a des choses que tu ne peux pas comprendre, he says —
whip's lightning, spinning top clearing the road,

miniature cyclones in the weather system of noonday traffic.

— *Un objet secret?* I ask.

— *Rien, non, rien de secret.*

. . . *Pose ta plume, parle-moi,* he says, *tu te souviendras.*

Mangue

He turns the fruit against the knife,
    good, stony weight   lending itself
        to remembrance
                (*Maison rouge*, he says, Eugénie, Adèle)

        names the ones he knows
      from the island's markets
          (Dauphine, Josée, Auguste)

the ones plucked
    without profit   (*Lacorde*)
        stringy and sweet   pulped in skin
      for a pouchful of sun
        to slurp

and the anonymous ones, stolen
    from someone's garden,
        lost when the tree dies
      fragrance   like a vanished language
            (roses, perhaps   ginger)

In Toronto, he snubs the supermarket
    Florida's Tommy Atkins
        goes instead
      to Little India, Chinatown, the Caribbean grocer

    for Alphonsos, Julies, Ataulfos

            encountering the city through its mangoes

Knife tucked against palm
        he holds his fingers round
                imaginary bodies,
   describes their shape

     heavy and globular
           or small, tapered   *comme une souris*

       the ones best eaten green, with salt and chili
       or at the point
       of silky ripeness

     their varied skins
          flecked, blushed, blazed

Red spiral of peel hangs round
        the fruit, paper lantern whose light
              is flesh   (*Rosa*)

   and he slices   a cheek

His guileless habit
   of bringing the knife to his lips

        yellow grin of mango
          on the blade

Pomme

Un objet donné?

Eh bien —

He was forbidden to speak to his father in Créole, but once,
when he was six, playing in the garden with his friend,
    his father called to him

language shimmered on his tongue like a fever

If he answered in French, his friend would think him strange, *un snob*,
would shun him; if he answered in Créole, he would be
    punished

he chose Créole

remembers the switch's whipped syllables, swift,
faultless, welts rising like letters
    on his bare back —

Next morning his mother kept him home from school,
    tongue-lashed her husband;
at noon he closed the clinic, knocked
at his son's bedroom door, told him to accompany him
    to town

they stopped at the cinema: bought two tickets
to *Les Trois Diables Rouges*, a Western starring Herman Brix,
    parts I and II

At intermission, his father brought out a brown paper bag

      inside,

two sweet red apples, imported from France, one for each of them;
taught him to rub the apple on his sleeve

til it shone —

Sansons

In another life, he says, he would've wanted to be a singer

Early music, the azan descending, in between the hours
of Lucienne Boyer, rosewater-sweet voice, hazy, woozy piano,
swirling from the gramophone

His first concert, Charles Trenet at the Plaza de Rose Hill —
grandest theatre in the Indian Ocean — Trenet leaving, amidst
the shouts for autographs, arm-in-arm with a young Muslim man
from the audience —
(*Ça aussi, tu vas écrire, bonhomme?* he exclaims,
as I scribble this down)

Séga on the radio, husky rhythm of the ravane, maravane, triangle,
reinvented decades later through drum brain, wah-wah pedal,
Moog and mini-Moog

Record collection crowded with the music hall singers,
the poets, the *comédiens*: Brassens' *Chanson de l'Auvergnat*,
to which he waltzes, slowly, one hand on belly, the other to
empty air
or Brel's *Ne me quitte pas*, which he sings in gruff giggles
so as not to weep

Acquainted with every version of Yves Montand's *À Paris*,
following its lovers and suicides down the Seine, down
the accordion's descant

Oui, oui, j'ai vu Louis Armstrong au Royal Albert Hall, remembers
the famous white handkerchief, Satchmo's exchange

with trombonist Trummy Young in *Rockin' Chair,* surprised
at the singer's speaking voice,
        sweeter, less rough than he'd imagined

    et Ella Fitzgerald à Dublin, au cinéma — the Ambassador,
je crois — the way she lilted *thank-you, thank-you,* at the end of
each song, birdlike, a grace note:
        Je la vois maintenant quand je l'écoute, he says,
          je la vois qui chante

    Seeing Charles Aznavour in Toronto, is moved
by the prelude to a love song, the singer miming a woman's
embrace — *comme ça* — my father turns away, wraps his arms
round himself, caresses
        the nape of his neck

Most often, sings on the go, uptempo, cheeky, clucking
his tongue, chuffing and making up Créole rhymes to keep time —
        Oh the shark has — *ti-gâteau-chéri-l'amour* —
          pretty teeth, dear — *ti-gâteau-co-co!* . . .

    Every now and then, after dinner, while we clear the table
or put the children to bed, he sings, gentle, grave,
        eyelids soft and heavy, half-closed

    In the morning, gargled slow song in the shower, water
strumming his back; razor's harmony to his absent-minded hum,
        electric ghazal

Scrabble

In the darkened house, light, flinty sounds, soft spark
of insomnia.

Pyjamaed intellectual, pillow-propped;
woody giggle and chatter of tiles, in their crushed
velvet Crown Royal pouch;

dictionary's fluttered lisp.

Far from the social game, the sun-sequined shade
of the mango tree, he and his friends
arguing in Créole, playing in English.

(His best: WALTZING — the T a given, W and G
hopscotched from one triple-word score to another,
the Z, 10-point pirouette on a double-letter score —
329 points!)

Closer to solitaire, language murmuring over the humdrum
of memory.

He lines up the tiles on the rack, pouts
with concentration, fist under chin, thumb
pressed to lips. And then

the play: letters soft-shoe, scuffle into place.
He scatters out new ones.

If I said his name, he would start — a half-snored, half-
  hiccuped sound — we would talk in shushed tones
  until he ushered me away, *bonne nuit!*

If I stand here, in the door frame, I can watch
  the gesture take form in the lamplight:

each tile, considered by touch, now waxy,
  coffee-brown as his own hand. The dark crease
  inscribed in his palm, a letter.

Zistoires

First memory of memory

suitcases   upended furniture

    an open crate

   in the new house   I hold my mother's skirt
      she comes down to the parquet
      knees smooth as opals or coddled eggs

        sinks her hands into straw   finds unfurls a scroll
            Oh, je me souviens du jour! . . .   she exclaims

   and gives me this memory
      a blue day, and me   walking home with
          an armful of selves
    portraits on craft paper a child's thumb-whorled signature
          in caked paint

I don't remember   frown at my mother
     her invention of me

   the one who made these drawings
        like the new girl you're asked to befriend
      full of wisdom in another tongue

Fledging

The bird twists from the egg, skin translucent
as rice paper. Spine
made of more light than bone;
an ink stain of heart.

He lifts it from ground, where it lies, hatched
by hatchet of wind. It opens
its beak: hisses: no song hinged
on this breath.

✦

The house hems the edge of the ravine, pins of sunlight
gleaming between its lips.

There are no adults, none without
their wonderless know-how. He takes
the bird to his little sister, shows her
their small task.

They forage through their father's cabinet, find
an eyedropper; mash worms and centipedes, dip
the glass tongue into its gullet, crow
to see it swallow;

wait for the thrill of quills beneath its skin.

✦

At night they nestle it in a shoebox,
an old shirt, some twigs.

She sleeps in the cricket-quilted dark,
but the boy returns, shining
his flashlight. The beam suspends the organs,
phosphorescent red, blue, in the bird's clear
body. Tiny black stars traverse
towards its wakeful eye, to sip: beetles.

✦

There are no adults, none with
their equivocal caches of chloroform.

It is up to him; both of them believe this.

He fills the washbasin.

He could simply let it sink. Instead he holds it
under, as though he were drowning a man.
She thinks the bird seems clearer
in water. Its head tilts back
towards white ceramic, loosening
a blister of air.

Fingers unclench. He feels betrayed, returns the bird
to the surface, half-drowned: mercy
clotted in his hand.

✦

She follows him, lurching against his heels like a wagon
as he heads to the green.

The ravine levels with him, the murmured tones
of leaves, wind, river. His stride
quickens; in mid-arc, he disowns
his fist, releases
the bird. The full-fledged earth flies upwards.

✦

She castles her chest, shy
before his *élan*, the ardent arc of his arm, all
the child burned away by grief;

his thin shoulders a marvel, holding
hurting and being hurt
like scapulae, wings.

Home remedy

"Garlic is as good as ten mothers."
— *Telugu saying*

Spied the first bulb in the living room, as I turned
away from the piano, imperfect scales, octaves
too wide for my hands. There
among all the knick-knacks collected
on the windowsill — seashells, a blown glass paperweight,
some misshapen bowl one of us made for her
when we were smaller.

I might have explained it to myself
thinking she'd walked away from her cooking
to open the window. Except
she no longer cooked: spent days in slumber, nights
in capricious wakefulness, hands now
constantly trembling. When she reached
to comb her fingers through my hair,
I flinched.

The second bulb I found by the shoes at the front door.
I took it back to the kitchen, not liking
things out of place: cloves
like so many eyes, closed, eyelids
fine as vellum, veined with violet.

My great-aunt's cookbook keeps a concoction
for cough syrup, made from garlic, fennel, sugar.
When my brother was stung by wasps,
it was crushed garlic we rubbed

on his swollen skin. There are so many uses.
She left bulbs on the balcony, at the edge
of the garage, near the skis and bicycles,
guarding all the entrances to her house,
her self, her family,
from revenants and werewolves.
Sticky juice smelling like the garter snake
I captured late that summer, secreting acrid milk in fear
and warning. I threw it away.

Once, as I pulled my nightgown over my head,
a single clove fell from the sleeve. I felt its skin
separate between my fingers: held it,
brittle as the wings of dragonflies, febrile
angels. Her daughter safe, my mother

flew from our house.

Girl, rabbit

Fully grown, she seemed bigger than her rabbit smallness. Ears, tail, paws tucked in, her body spilled and settled beyond her, a white farthingale. Fur doubled at the chin, an Elizabethan collar: ruffs like lettuce. Ruby eyes glittered. She gazed imperially over her dominion, towards other continents, seeing neither. She saw me. My small-mouthed, small-boned determination. She did not trust me.

✦

Her name did not fit her: one of those terms of endearment recalling white clouds in springtime. She gnashed her teeth and made indignant, piggy grunts. When I let her out, she caromed across the living room; in her cage, retreated to a corner, glared redly my way. Thumped. Sneezed, ire peppering her nostrils.

I bargained for her forgiveness with celery hearts and strawberries, though twice (once to see, and once to show my brother) I fed her a chili. She nursed scalded taste buds for an hour after. She loved salt from my hand, though never coming too close — straining to touch her tongue to the crush on my fingertips.

✦

The irrepressible instinct to chew: chair and table legs, telephone wires, the upright piano, the Oxford English Dictionary, my father's vinyl collection, the heels of my mother's sandals. Broom bristles left behind when my mother shook the broom at her.

The instinct to burrow: tear away grass, score the earth, dig. A place where she was held without hands, sunshine rimming the entrance. Early on she went further, burrowed past the makeshift fence of picnic chairs. Then my family and I searched for the comma shape of her, now a white dash in the greenery of suburbs.

These burrows hurt me. I reached to their centre, felt their promise of home. Their wish for elsewhere.

✦

I bought a leash that I tied to the maple tree, leaving her to nibble blades of grass in summer, root out their frozen shoots in winter.

Once, I heard a wild, high whistling, ran out to the balcony to see her and the neighbour's cat in helical chase, radius of flight tightening with every circuit round the tree. I shooed the cat away, but her screaming continued for several seconds, breath forced through an unknown organ. As if fear were a syrinx, a muscle reserved for one vowel, one song.

✦

The instinct to pull fur. She sat back on her haunches, combed her belly with front paws, caressed a slight skein into being. It floated as if in wait, the cage gleaming, amniotic, until strand by strand it came undone and disappeared.

✦

I knelt, nestled her between my thighs. She slipped, hopped
away; I plopped her back, smoothed her taut ears. She darted.
Claws rasped as I grasped her by the haunches. She bit, breaking
skin. I squeezed her head down, spanked her across flank. She
became still, trembling. I pinned her with one hand, petted her
with the other *love me love me love me* . . .

✦

I gave her a stuffed toy, a pink elephant. She brushed it with
whiskers, nuzzled it; it tipped over and showed its white rump.
She tapped it, one paw, then the other. Rolled it. Suddenly
mounted it, almost falling over as she thrust against it in
increasing rhythm. Cage thrummed, a discordant piano.
Vegetable pellets added their tambourine rattle. Water in the
water bowl puckered, a liquid, quivering nipple. From beneath
her the elephant gazed at me, button eyes lumped together
each time she humped.

That summer I discovered masturbation, spent an entire Sunday
dizzying myself with fantasies of rape and ravishment *I want —
I don't care — anything* plummeting under the covers and coming.
My mother knocked: I rearranged the pillows and answered
weakly. I said I was sick. She put her hand to my forehead, found
me feverish, made me stay home from school the next day.

✦

Thinking she needed a companion, I bought another: black, with a white stripe on his nose. He made honking noises upon seeing her, but she would not be kindred: pushed the fruit I gave her through the grid into the dung balls below.

I kept them in separate cages, but let them loose together in the living room to play. He badgered and bragged, tail a flag on hind legs held high. Not quite her size, he pinioned her. Startled her, though she didn't pull away. Their bodies thinned with muscularity and intent. I knelt to separate them. She fluttered beneath him. He leapt at me. Teeth clamped into palm, white electrodes. I stood and raised my arm and he hung on, wriggling in mid-air before letting go.

✦

The instinct to pull fur. She combed her belly, loosened the strands. Under the Christmas tree she wove a nest of tinsel and fur. Sat, fat and content as a creamer.

✦

I never saw the kindling.

✦

Blind for the first days, the kits were guided by heat. If I held them up to my face, they sought out the moisture of breath. If I stuck out my tongue, they grasped for it, and finding the tip, suckled.

✦

They had no scent of their own. She granted them hers: licked their soft bodies, slicked a path to her teats. Let me stroke them.

The day we gave them to the local kindergarten, I brought her blackberries. She nudged them aside, licked my fingers, sniffed the creases of my palm.

✦

Sounds in the middle of the night woke me. A metallic clamour. I walked down in the dark. The male reared up on hind legs, gnawed and grunted at the grid. She crouched in her cage, whimpering. A to-and-fro sound. Rocking. I never saw the kindling. The kits were dead. She rolled one beneath her paws like a rolling pin, its body bruised and bloodied from the pressure of wire and claws. The nest of fur I'd failed to notice already disintegrating.

✦

The black one became increasingly territorial, once bulling me til I jumped onto a chair. I took his cage to the garden, unlatched the door, walked away without looking back. At night, a thunderstorm. Outside, I found a glistening bundle. Gelatinous from rain. From blood. It reminded me of the colours of licorice. He had wandered into the neighbour's yard: when the cat gave chase, he had run back towards the safety of the cage, but the door swung the wrong way. Stranded, he'd been slashed open, clean as a raincoat.

✦

If I lay on my belly in the grass, she would come near and likewise, lay herself low. Eye to eye, nose to nose, we were paper dolls unfolded at the crown.

The doe's instinct to pull fur, as though she could make nestlings as she made a nest. I thought of her making me, beginning with tresses, eyelashes. Hairs raised from gooseflesh. Licking me from head to toe to recognize my scentless body.

As I grew older, she receded from my view, small. At fifteen, I pushed at the thin stretch of earth between me and sky, adjusted my eyes to the light brimming above. Wild field of adolescence, waiting.

Goodness

The season of visits to the hospital
I would not look at her, instead
traced the grout between
pale green tiles, blew
breath figures against glass.

When she called home, collect —
   Do you accept the charge? —
I said no, slammed the receiver
into the cradle,
her pleading a winged insect in a jar.

I played mother, cleaned house,
did laundry, washed dishes,
ironed, forged her signature
on my report cards;

learned to make beds with hospital corners,
sheets tucked in twice, kept taut
until morning.

My body leaned its weight
into counters and floors, shoulderblades
a silent, bony argument —

good girl, good girl, vengeful in goodness —

scrubbing the house of the smell of her cooking,
the rougaille, caramelized tomatoes,

garlic and ginger, thyme,
displaced now
by artificial pine.

Still she recognized me, loved, reached
    for me: bright and gleaming
in my rage, a new coat
I wore with pride.

Mercury

Midnight, and I am standing in waste: dumpster
of green-painted plywood and chicken wire.
Beneath the street lamp, a glinting cloud
of moths and mayflies;
three flights up, you pace the circle
of lamplight in the living room.
I want to tell you I'm sorry.

Somewhere here is a cylinder of toxin
I've thrown out by mistake. You chided me,
then thought of my hands finding
splintered glass, heavy, metallic drops.
Let me come down with you,
you said, but I was bent
on fighting: *No use in both of us . . .*

I tumble plastic bags away from me, wondering
if it will have snapped: spill of blue-
black beads, *dragées* on wedding cakes.
Ascent into air, then the spores' slow shower;
sink into lake, lungs. The mirrored cells
of fish.

To think this may come from a thermometer,
that we place under our tongues
— soft trove — with our first
syllable, kiss, stolen anise. In fevered
nights, the lean of parents, bodies
dark in the amber doorway. *Ouvre la bouche.*
Glass in the mouth, against the teeth,

ne mords pas. The instrument
lifted to the light, tilted, so its milky facet
becomes lucent. The reading of degrees,
so slight; the measure of disquiet.

I find it, whole, come back upstairs,
and still, our relief tainted: my silence,
shoulders curved inward.
       Four a.m. Outside, raised voices.
From separate beds, we come to the window.
Police's beacon sheens the street. We watch
for a moment. *Come back to bed.*
You close the window, let the night
come in; moonlight tilted through the blinds,
falling in silver across our feet.

Depression as curio

There is some comfort in knowing it is handed down,

retrieved from the place
she came back from. There is comfort
in the imprint it carries, slant light
of a seaside window, rainy scent
of another climate.

      Decipher its use
by its shape, its mechanics: what locks,
unlocks; what twists and clicks; what
opens. Whether it makes a sound.

I want it to be stone, to be iron.

The gesture it requires. The habit with which
you pick it up, turn it over,
revisit it. Small possession, with its specific,
secret history.

I am thinking of hands. Hers. Amber-
coloured, long-fingered, bones like bamboo,
the frame of a kite. What she has known
before me, what her father, perhaps, knew before her.
Passed, without touch, without words, between
us. The heat of her hand. The coolness of mine.

Field of vision

My father softens, a garment without its body,
hangs the weight of his head on the chinrest; peers
into a globe to the screen like a wide, shallow bowl.
Points of light in a diamond-shaped pattern
wink, green, random. On the monitor,
in black and white, an image of
his iris darts in the frame.

The ophthalmologist touches a key, begins
the visual field test. Here
is an encapsulated sky, where night is reversed,
white and shining with technical stars;
here, a constellation without mythology, repeated
while the dot matrix printer annotates his vision.

✦

Small yellow pear kisses cornea; pupil, beguiled.

The slit lamp's silver light moves
across his face like the crack of a door opening.
The doctor crowns himself with the ophthalmoscope,
a miner's helmet: cobalt
soaks a pocket of dark,
my father suddenly blue-eyed.

Glaucoma:
            chroma
        of silver bloom on blue plums, the hour
        entre chien et loup, when red thread
        is bled of colour.

        ✦

I drive him back, steering wheel's breastbone
between my hands.

Sun's late light flares across the sky; he receives it
kaleidoscopic. He says: once, coming home,
he turned a corner and drove straight into
the moon, fallen onto our street: *là*,
cracked by horizon, molten and pouring
into road's asphalt. Remembers heart-pound,
how he swerved, slammed on the brakes, mind
grasping for clutch of reason: then,
the real's unperturbed shift back into place:

only moon rising,

gravid with light from the other side of earth.

Fulcrum

Early spring, earth blooms through melting snow.
We are driving to a small town, a church, the funeral
of Sheila's father: you at the wheel, me scanning
the signs, green, metallic blinks
against my eyes. Late, lost.

Finally you take an exit, a gravel road, a bridge
passing over an undulating field. The map unfolds
in a crinkly mutter of explanations.
     A shadow touches your hand. I look up:
eye level, an arm's length from the car, suspended —
red-tailed hawk.
          How . . . ?
               We are at the bridge's edge, hawk
scooping the updraft from the valley below, still
except for the slight swivel and stop
of its head. *Look!* But you
are reading the map— *not now* — eyes gem-cut
with impatience, that we are not where we should be.

So it's me and the hawk. Windshield between us,
I watch the russet-feathered breast;
quills outstretched, not a wingbeat, only the quiver
and control of muscle calibrating air.
     I have a flash of doing a handstand
on a unicycle — *like that* — wind
a fulcrum, silver wheel, circus ball. Then

a slackening, the hawk tilts back, thermal taking it
higher. Its companion swoops into view, and the two
plane, one over the other, a pair of hands
holding cat's cradle. Separate;
I twist against the seat belt to watch them
lift, flow over us, away.

As we double back, I lean
into the sureness of your direction, elated as we pass
red osier dogwood, staghorn sumac,
seed heads like musical notation along the road. Thinking
of the ceremony we have missed, Sheila
encircled by friends; how we will meet
her eyes as we step into the church, this sighting
a story I'll wait to tell her.

Shells, stones

The seashells line the illuminated glass shelves:

thin-spined murex, knobby conch and tapered whelk,
heart-shaped cockle and strombid's claw,
      cowries in child's pose.

       Many of them found
on seaside walks, where we showed them to each other,
delighting in their shapes, their colours:
      striated, splotched,
            doodled, scribbled, lettered,
    the one with a landscape
          of mountains and valleys, the orange-stained one,
as though adorned with henna.

There's a theory they make these patterns through toxins
secreted from mantle, what would otherwise
      cause harm, laid down
   in vivid geometry
         (the design of sorrow,
something we want to believe in).

Here, we translated seashell to lake stone, seashell
            to basalt,
granite, rhyolite,
      gabbro and gneiss; walked
with the same habit, heads bent, lowering to lustre,
        the partial swell in sand.

When my parents returned to the island, I stood at the edge
of the lake, as though they were simply on the other side
of that body of water.

Wanting them back

for that walking, singly, then
that gathering round
stone or blossomed bone in an open palm.

First memory of reading

we sit together   open the book   to a clearing
                in a forest
    suited and booted bears   foxes in scarves   mittened rabbits

safe and sound, she reads
                    words' sibilance   a secret
        passage from one language   to another

                sain et sauf!   I exclaim
                    and she hugs me   closer

one shape nestled into the other
        book tucked in my body
                my body tucked in hers

                her pollen-golden hand on mine
        a clasp

Poems for the Advisory Committee on Antarctic Names

"*Considering that it has no permanent residents, it seems surprising that Antarctica has more than 14,000 official names, all pondered over by committees . . . It is here that you have the best chance of having a geographic feature named after you, but only if you are an expedition leader or have performed some heroic act on the ice . . .*"

— The New Scientist

◆

We descend into colour dense with earth. Ochre, on bicycle wheels, buses' exhaust, sandalled feet.

¿Cómo se dice —? The Spanish that I once learned eludes me: the word for coin, the one for custom. Hands tender pamphlets, election's slogans. *Soy contigo:* I am with you.

My older brother walks ahead, carrying my knapsack. All day, some memory of his boyhood tags me, hoists a song he used to sing off-key: *Hissé-oh, Santiago!* In the Mercado, a man leans into our conversation, drops a pebble of Latin-accented French. Our mother tongue a well where we keep our childhood. He tells us he learned the language in exile during Pinochet's terrors. He is a beekeeper, cultivates their honey, the medicine of their sting; carries living, golden bees from his farm. Inside transparent drums, they hum: I hold one to my ear.

In the plaza, the Communist party demonstration becomes a concert, crowds dancing. Flags gash the horizon, wring the last vermilion from the sky.

♦

In the southernmost city on earth, all messages wing north. The post office is a rookery, clamouring with voices, blurted interjections of packing tape; cyber-cafés with the tongue-cluck, teeth-kiss of keyboards. In separate kiosks, Yousouf and I call home: he to his wife and baby girl, I to my husband; each of us trellised against the other's reflection.

Ushuaia.

In the city whose Yaghan name means simply, the bay that opens towards the end, we walk to the harbour. Watch the seabirds gather in the indigo dusk, a flock of signals, binary in black and white, angled in another direction. Further, they say, as they lift their wings, pry open the south.

✦

The door nudges a dangling bell. In a five-room house turned into a museum, a woman at a writing desk takes my pesos; another parts the calico curtain to let me in.

On the map of an old continent, a dashed line like teeth marks: human passage. Fossilized light of lithographs, photographs. A basket. A reinvention of the Yaghan canoe: bone, sinew, beech bark. They lowered them to water, once, fire in the hull held safe in hands of moss and clay.

Not far, Argentina's penal colony, six-pointed star that studs Tierra del Fuego. Portraits of the criminals and dissidents who built modern Ushuaia's scaffolding of myth. Excerpts of the writings of poets and essayists sent here. Nothing of the women: white women imported to create a European population; Aboriginal women who married white men when their own died. They mouth their histories, a narrative of signs and silences.

Yousouf has been here before, so I walk through by myself, trailing a stranger, the stranger sometimes trailing me.

✦

On board, Yousouf joins the crew as doctor. Quizzing the passengers, he sheds the eldest son's brown coat, shines with a curiosity vivid as a kingfisher.

In the library at the ship's bow, I grip the table, try to anchor the armchair with my weight. Books slide away, each sentence a tilting skyline: reading becomes vertiginous.

Sleep, too, swills in our heads, decants into our toes. In the night, sun mints coins upon our closed eyelids.

(I enter through his eye, kingfisher eye quicker than mine, slow, dreaming. He is the explorer, found the hatchling, the wasp's nest. When we went walking on the beach, I found sea urchin spines, the ones you could write on your slate with, and cowrie shells. Drab things. He found the finger of blue coral. Blue, like a blue vein, or the blue lips of a child come in from the cold. He gave it to our mother. I stood on tiptoe to see into her palm: *Je peux voir? Ah*, she said, *c'est beau.*)

✦

All the sky's greys mineralize to birds: kohl-eyed
albatross; black agate Cape petrel, Wilson's storm petrel;
galena-sheened Antarctic prion.

Bones hollowed for flight, weighted for diving, wing translated
from air to sea.

We learn to tell whether they'll sweep or stab
the wave. We learn the shape of
the breath of whales: bushy cloud of the orca, heart-shaped blow
of the grey; the bowing exhalation of minkes. They roll
in the distance, black cardamom pods.
Tail,
a keyhole on the horizon.

✦

Icebergs: tabular, dome, pinnacle.

The continent opens its mouth: slow, Antarctic stutter, cleft palate
syllables of snow.

✦

On the leaden sea, from each prism, a blue, luminous
hum.

✦

We goat-head into the wind, zero point five knots
north-west, only
to hold our position. Caesura. Before
a vast white wall, we work ourselves up to
some kind of wisdom.

✦

Sun spools in the southern sky.

Lifejacket; snowsuit; gloves, balaclava, gumboots. Turtled, I push
my head into the clear; the landscape rides me
piggyback.

Hood rims my vision in a bright orange corona. Red sea kelp. Rose
jellyfish. A trace of teal-green copper oxide in stone. Hennaed
handprints of lichen. The footprints we make in firn snow
linger, blue.

✦

Crab-eater seals crane their necks towards us. We drift forward
through frazil ice in the Zodiac, smiles sprigging
a bouquet of binoculars and cameras.

They smile back — by which I mean, their lips slope upwards.
Rubbery pun. We love this, this recognition of a gesture.
Of ourselves.

(On the tail of one, the cicatrix of an orca's chomped grin.)

✦

Penguins spat from the sea, seeds from the lips
of watermelon seed-spitting champions.

We follow their cocktail-shrimp-pink trails of
pooped krill, stink of saltfish curry
and briny kazoo calls.

Anthropomorphism
a Jack-in-the-box that won't stay put:

Adélies, googly-eyed, as though caught red-
handed, stealing from the bulk bins; chinstraps,
no-nonsense French gendarmes; macaronis
in their fez hats and European suits.

They blot their warmth against their
eggs, bow, beak each other in
symmetrical affection.

Swift swim like the twang of a steel guitar —

And us, in our artificial plumage, walking in an eyeful huddle:
a singular species.

◆

Gentoo penguins, collegial, bark greetings; one, a customs agent, inspects the kayaks.

Inside the Vernadsky research station: X-ed calendars; Crayola salutes of children; the Virgin's turquoise robes, gold haloes and sugar pink tunics of angels; pin-ups of women in American cars; charts measuring Indonesia's tsunami, Kashmir's earthquake.

Maps of the ozone hole, weird glaucoma.

In the gift shop, a baroque crow rises from an illustrated version of *The Snow Queen*. Home movies, showing the researchers playing soccer; penguins watching, heads nodding as if to a bouncing-ball sing-along cartoon; and the cook who's taught himself to move one eye independently of the other.

How many of you are here? Yousouf asks the young Ukrainian geophysicist. Straight-faced, he answers: Eighteen men: no woman: no cry.

✦

Yousouf smooths a snowball, sends it in a clear arc over the stone-eyed water of the bay.

(There, again — Hissé-oh!)

On the far shore, a leopard seal lifts its massive head, gazes peaceably at my brother.

◆

Spectrum sharpened to shadow and mirror, melded onto a single blade.

Glitter of brash ice like metal, chrome instruments on the aseptic sea.

A white room:
asylum.

In the water, torn jaw of a whale, what is left of an orca pod's kill: smooth throat

grooves turned towards the surface, tendrils of flesh, a lily in bloom.

✦

A Weddell seal, mercurial, slips through a corridor of
growlers, pink and green quartzite:

snout, pot-belly, flipper.

Or hump of back.

As though
only one part of its body lives at a time.

As though
it is separate bodies changing form and formation.

As though
it lives in two worlds.

Glazed water won't let you see, sends your gaze
back to you.

✦

Horizon pulls: a trick knot, the seal undoes itself.

✦

Throat song:

Skuas whistle over the colonies, harmonic intervals of
cloud, crag, crèche.

Threat caresses penguins, as they stand amidst their kind's
carcasses, ransacked: wings, coat hangers
flung from the rack, skin the inside-out coat;

broken-into eggs, meringues of blood and rainwater.

In the shallows below, a droning undertone: leopard seals.

✦

Longline fishing:

its many hooks, a single leading question: an interrogation.

Fibrous water rasps seabirds below.

We find a dead skua,

garbled with fishhook and wire,
claw, frozen, unable to rot.

✦

Last year, it was my father accompanying Yousouf. High summer
on the peninsula, season of hatchlings and pups, grass on
the northerly islands gone to purply-reddish seed.

For days he was disappointed that the whales swam so far from
the ship, that he knew them only by cambered silhouette,
the moment between breath and dive.

On the crossing to land, a minke surfaced next to the Zodiac.
The crew slowed, sputtered to a halt. Pointed head, glossy, dark
blue, so close he could touch it.

     Curve, eye, blink.

          Bonjour, Monsieur.

On another island, he and Yousouf walked through flowering
grass, the keel of a whale's ribcage; knelt beside two fused
vertebrae,

     consulted, confirmed

          their diagnosis: arthritis.

✦

The cruise ship, once used for Soviet reconnaissance, is still manned by a Russian engineering crew. A Russian doctor shares the clinic with Yousouf, to look after his compatriots. Without a common language, he nonetheless converses with us daily, without pause or explanation: sheer enthusiasm a fail-safe against mistranslation.

At each landing, he uncases his video camera, holds it at arm's length, places himself squarely in its sights. Addresses it quietly as though revealing a life-long secret, presumably something of the *Here-I-am-standing* . . . variety, in the valvular sounds of Slavic.

Towards the last day, he invites us back to his cabin. Pulls out a banker's box packed with video tapes; plays us one, then another, then another. In each, what is foregrounded is his marvelling face, a thin scarf of landscape flapping round his ears.

I lend him my notebook. Dollar signs, his salary in Russia; he hands the notebook to Yousouf. My brother hesitates, then, pen quickening, mimics him. "But — " he adds. Draws a house, a stick-figure family, a hump with wheels for a car: the cost of living. I catch his eye; his gaze flickers.

Genially, the Russian doctor points to his stethoscope, then to Yousouf's, wags his fingers between them. In friendship, he means. To remember each other. He cocks his head. Yes? Yousouf smiles, nods. They trade.

Later, when we're alone, Yousouf tests the Russian doctor's stethoscope, shakes his head, a kind of sympathy, a kind of shame. He will purchase a new one in Toronto.

✦

In between islands, I return
          to the ship's reading room, find
                    a history of Tierra del Fuego.

A boy for a mother-of-pearl button. Nothing
          of the mother, running across pearl slopes,
                    to keep her son in sight.

Orundellico, Yockushlu, Elleparu:
          children taken from Ushuaia. Punishment
                    for the theft of a whaling boat,

a button pressed into the hand
          makes it trade. (An anger so pure, clear,
                    vaporous, it forgets itself instantly.)

They are returned without their names,
          Jemmy Button, Fuegia Basket, York Minster,
                    named again for worth, a curio, nostalgia;

they speak a new language where *I*
          is always the same, the same.

A young and unknown biologist accompanies them
          home, will rewrite one story
                    of origin, but what about stories

of return: where you come to the doorway
          of your name, and the door is no longer there, the house
                    is no longer there?

✦

Boat Memory.

Two words inscribed in a hospital ledger,
      each sentence a tilting skyline,
            no translation will return him

to himself. Boat Memory dies of smallpox
      and you say the only name
            he is known by, rocking

its ambiguity on your tongue, feeling
      for the scar on its strange eloquence.
            His story surfaces

as flotsam, jetsam; marker, if not exactly
      of place, at least of event. It doesn't tell you
            where something sank, only

the currents, the tides that have made it drift
      away, since.

Orundellico, Yockushlu, Elleparu.
      Jemmy Button, Fuegia Basket, York Minster.
      Boat Memory.

You wonder what he is named for, his memory
      of a boat, or a boat's
            memory of him?

Who remembers?
        Who is remembered?
            The book slides away.

That spellbound unknowing, between question
    and answer —

✦

Whale bone, boat hull: what is left
    exhaled by ocean, unnatural,
        onto shores of shale.

On an island named Deception, caldera, cauldron,
    ash-layered glacier, rivers of
        meltwater and black shining mud.

Whalebone, boat hull: wood, bone, dulled.
    How alike they are: porous, greyed
        and roughened;

I press my hand to each body. How
    they come to the same state:
        inflammation of lichen,

flare of pale green,
    vivid orange (even decay
        wants to live).

Whalebone, boat hull. *Boat Memory.*
    Stranded, boat remembers whale,
        whale remembers boat;

the mining of a living, blue-black ore,
    the first off-shore drilling operation,
        the process of dismemberment called

    rendering   to melt down, to clarify,   to express.

Sea lulls bone, hull; seaweed
　　washed ashore, parting sand and sea, red
　　　　as sindoor powder through a woman's hair.

Rale of wind in rusted lungs
　　in the cauldrons,
　　　　in the hall of the whale's ribs.

Whalebone, boat hull: constellation
　　of a holocaust, and still,
　　　　beauty, beauty,

blue water against red earth,
　　red earth against blue sky.

✦

Oh —

he is the thief.

     Boat Memory, named
          so he will not forget.

               Reading becomes vertiginous.

✦

An open sea:
　　　an open book.
　　　　　A photograph

of an incidental island: *"A whale*
　　　marked by a flag and left floating while another
　　　　　is pursued. Note

the leaden sky and bright distant land."

　　　　　(A white room: asylum.)

On the floating stations, men flense the whales,
　　　step into the body's cradle, to cut
　　　　　deeper.

　　　　　(The glitter of metal.)

Wash their hands in warm blood to save them
　　　from frostbite. The visiting doctor reports
　　　　　land stations to be *"the most sordid,*

unsanitary habitation
　　　of white men to be found
　　　　　the whole world over . . ."

An open sea:
　　　blue, right, humpback, sperm, minke, fin,
　　　　　sei.

✦

In a museum farther north is the only recording of the Yaghan tongue. Ferns of language pressed into the soft wax cylinders of an Edison phonograph, recorded a century ago. Their grammar integrated perspective. Your name would be different if I called to you from a canoe, or from the shore; your name would be different if earth or water lay between us.

✦

Boom.

A glacier calves. Sometimes, the captain says, the sound reaches
you after, the way thunder does after lightning: your brain fizzes
and pops as it recalibrates its sense of distance, magnitude.

The nature of that break, crown driving down, exploding
its anchor. The hyper-clarity of it, tracing the fault in pure blue.

Your face falls.

(In the hour before cyclone's landfall, the sky darkens to hematite red. Wind rises. Yousouf and I are an arm's length away from each other, a child's arm: testing the wind against our bodies, our voices. We lean into it and it does not let us fall; we scream each other's names, and it takes their sounds, leaves nothing but their shape like empty bottles, and our wide-eyed, wide-mouthed laughter. We inhabit each other and wind inhabits us; this is as far as we have ever travelled. The weather system advances, bends and sweeps the palm trees to make a Sanskrit alphabet. Our mother is calling, calling us in.)

✦

A tern beats its wings, hovers over its nest, a pulley strung with invisible ropes. Yousouf raises his camera, silhouette serifed against the snow.

A timber sign pins the emptiness: *British Crown Land*. How uneasy it makes us, this tensile connection between the name and the named. By a hut, white reaches for the red painted letters that spell *Wordie House*, the doorway already taken.

Petermann Island. Pléneau Island. Yalour. Lemaire Channel. Wilhemina Bay. Gerlache Strait. Neko Harbour.

How easily this place renounces its names, returns to namelessness. Listen. Don't say anything about the self. He on the shore, me on the hillside, we look up: the tern is indiscernible from sky.

Reading the
Yamana-English Dictionary

Reading the Yamana-English Dictionary

To open one's eyelids with one's hands, return
from the nod and drift to the subway's tug. Across
from me a man bends his head towards a book, the line
of his body refracted in reading's concentration. *To come up*

*to the head of a creek, inlet or river while running. To cross
over an open stretch of water, going westward. To reach
quiet waters among islands, coming from the sea.* Travelling
eastbound along the Bloor-Danforth line, across the bridge, over

the snow-filled river and its brace of highways. Travelling
while reading an old paperback, crow's feet crinkling
its night-blue face. Marvelling that there is a word for *eggs
without shells, as found in the interior of birds*

before the shell is formed. That the word for *dumb, unable
to speak, slow or stammering in speech,* is related to the one
for *glistening, bright, shiny. A bright burnished surface.*
The worlds created by parts of speech, but especially,

these verbs, their clarity, even as I have
no clear action of my own. *To grow up and forget
what one used to do, say or be like.* Their diversity,
and their loss, too: failed promise of the infinitive, gesture

severed from the body that signs it.

The man in the subway car stands, sways, as we pull through
the tunnel; a synthesized feminine voice announces
the station; not his; he sits down again. This whole movement
without lifting his eyes from the page.

In an oral culture, the words for writing: *To try to write. Unable*
to write, to never write, to write erroneously.
Words coined or reimagined to describe the foreigner,
stooped to his notebook in the vast landscape. How this language

multiplies intent: whether one does a thing occasionally,
cleverly, secretly; by mistake, whistling, in moonlight, alone
or in the company of others. The many words related to the canoe:
To be pleased in having a canoe of one's own to go about in.

Daydreamed walk home. From between the pages,
flicker of copper: a bookmark. A library slip, recording
this book and others borrowed with it, so I could trace
my way to another reader through her curiosity.

To write in a standing position. To write
here and there, irregularly, hurriedly.
To go on, with diligence,
your writing.

In the house across the street, a woman comes to the window
reading, draws the curtain, her head down. That gesture
again. *To be dreamt about, to be the subject*
of a dream. The key chirrups as it hatches

from your pocket, brass wing through the keyhole. You kiss me
hello. I tell you my favourite word: *To convert oneself,*
or be converted, into a bird. We wonder
about this together. How necessary

these words are, pebbles dropped into a glass, making
the water rise. When I am near
empty. *To wheel a barrow into the sea, lake,*
river, et cetera.

Glossary

agram-bagram: Créole for this and that.

Allé, éta, guette-il: go on, hey, look at him!

azan: the call to prayer.

brash ice: small, floating fragments of ice, the wreckage of other forms of ice.

Ça aussi tu vas écrire, bonhomme?: You're gonna write that down too, man?

comme une souris: like a mouse.

entre chien et loup: literally, between dog and wolf; a figure of speech for dusk.

filao: a species of pine tree.

firn snow: snow which has become granular and dense but has not yet become ice.

flamboyant: a species of flowering tree.

frazil ice: a collection of loose ice crystals in water, resembling slush.

growler: a small iceberg.

Il nous fallait être inventif: We had to be inventive.

Il y a des choses que tu ne peux pas comprendre: There are things you can't understand.

Je la vois maintenant quand je l'écoute, je la vois qui chante: I see her now when I hear her, I see her singing.

Mamzelle Pomme d'Amour, Missié Pistasse: Créole for Miss Love Apple, Mister Pistachio.

macaroni: a species of penguin. Other species mentioned: Adélie, chinstrap, and gentoo.

maravane: a gourd filled with small stones or dried nuts, a musical instrument used in séga.

mi, la mie d'un bon pain chaud: in French, the syllable "mi" is a homonym for the word that describes the soft interior of bread.

pistasse: Créole for pistachio.

pomme: apple.

Pose ta plume, parle-moi, tu te souviendras: Put down your pen, talk to me, you'll remember.

ravane: a hide drum, used in séga.

Rosa: a mango cultivated in Mauritius. Other cultivars named: Maison rouge (red house) and Lacorde (Créole for rope).

sanson: Créole for song.

séga: a Mauritian musical form, originating in songs and dances of African slaves during the French colonial period.

sindoor: a red powder applied along the parting line of a woman's hair.

skua: a predatory seabird.

un son clair: a clear sound.

zistoire: Créole for story.

Notes

The quotation that begins the fourth section is from *The New Scientist* and is reprinted with permission.

Some of these poems are based on research on the Yaghan or Yamana people of Tierra del Fuego and the whaling industry of the south seas. Orundellico, Yockushlu, and Elleparu are the Yaghan names of three of four children who were kidnapped in 1830 by British missionaries and taken from Ushuaia to England. The fourth, known only by his English name, Boat Memory, died of smallpox at the Naval Hospital in Plymouth, England. Orundellico, Yockushlu, and Elleparu were eventually returned to Ushuaia, accompanied by Charles Darwin. Jemmy Button was implicated in the massacre of British missionaries twenty-nine years later.

"Whale bone, boat hull" is inspired by a visit to Deception Island, the site of a whaling station abandoned in 1931. The quotation "A whale marked by a flag . . ." is from *Whaling in the Antarctic* by A.G. Bennett (Blackwood: Edinburgh, 1931). The quotation "the most sordid, unsanitary habitation . . ." is cited in *A History of World Whaling* by Daniel Francis (Viking: Ontario, Canada, 1990).

The phrases in italics in "Reading the Yamana-English Dictionary" are taken from *Yamana-English, A Dictionary of the Speech of Tierra del Fuego* by the Reverend Th. Bridges, a missionary and settler who lived between 1842 and 1898. Originally published by his children in 1933, the dictionary was republished in 1987 by Zaglier y Urruty Publicaciones, Buenos Aires, Argentina. The Yaghan language is nearly extinct; a recording made in the early 1900s exists in the Rauner Library at Dartmouth and in the Library of Congress.

Merci

My deepest thanks to George Elliott Clarke and Gerry Shikatani, mentors and friends, for their extended and generous support throughout the development of this work.

To my editor, Roo Borson, for her attentive eye and gentle hand. To the good people at Goose Lane Editions, especially Ross Leckie, guest editor Sharon McCartney, Akoulina Connell, and Julie Scriver.

To teachers at various workshops: Marilyn Dumont and Warren Cariou at the Sage Hill Writing Experience; rob mclennan; and John Steffler, also at Sage Hill, for his big-hearted response to early drafts of these poems. To other writers and editors for their encouragement: Hiro Boga at Oolichan Press, Margaret Christakos, Amanda Jernigan at *The New Quarterly*, and damian lopes.

To the editors of anthologies and journals where earlier versions of some of these poems appeared: *Red Silk: An Anthology of South Asian Canadian Women Poets* (Toronto: Mansfield Press, 2004), *Other Voices*, and *Prairie Fire*.

To the Canada Council for the Arts and the Ontario Arts Council Chalmers Professional Development Program and Works-in-Progress Program. To the recommenders who supported me through the OAC Writers' Reserve Program: Coach House Press, Kiss Machine, and Wolsak and Wynn.

To my colleagues at the University of Guelph MFA in Creative Writing program, especially Aisha Sasha John, Elisabeth de Mariaffi, and Erin Robinsong. To the late Constance Rooke, an extraordinary and indefatigable artist. I acknowledge the support of the Constance Rooke Harper Collins Scholarship; thanks to David Kent at Harper Collins.

Love and thanks to Anna Chatterton, Evalyn Parry, and Suzanne Robertson, who make writing such joy. Suzanne especially, for lending your keen eye and ear to these poems, and for all our correspondence and conversations about the words and experiences that move us. You inspire me. To Sheila Bhatacharya, Prasad Bidaye, and Helen Poisson.

Though I have thanked him above, I want to acknowlege again Gerry Shikatani, who has influenced not only craft but also practice; who befriended these poems and their materials, and taught me to attend to the poem's request. His editorial insights grace this work.

À ma famille, pour tous les paysages, réels et intérieurs, habités et racontés, que nous avons visités ensemble. To Mark, for our lives together, your rock-solid support, your belief and love. Et à Sheyla, d'être venue à notre rencontre.

Thank you.

Soraya Peerbaye has lived in Toronto and her ancestral home, Mauritius.

Her poetry has appeared in *Other Voices, Prairie Fire, The New Quarterly,* and in *Red Silk: An Anthology of South Asian Canadian Women Poets.*

Photo: G.H. Peerbaye